THIS NOTEBOOK BELONGS TO:

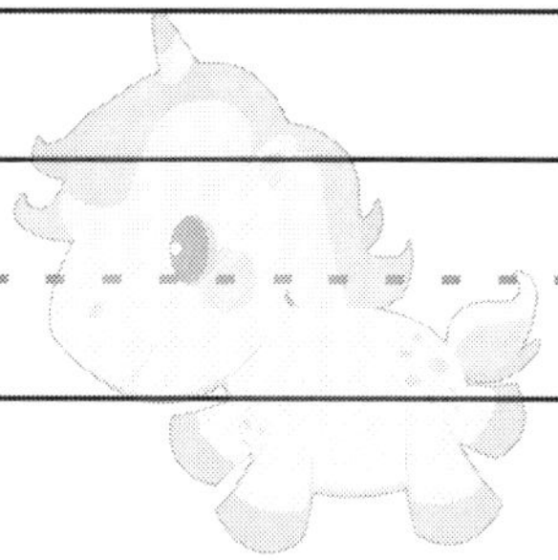

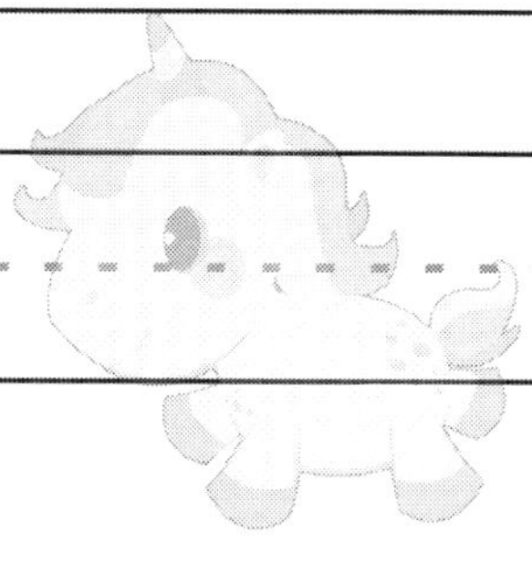

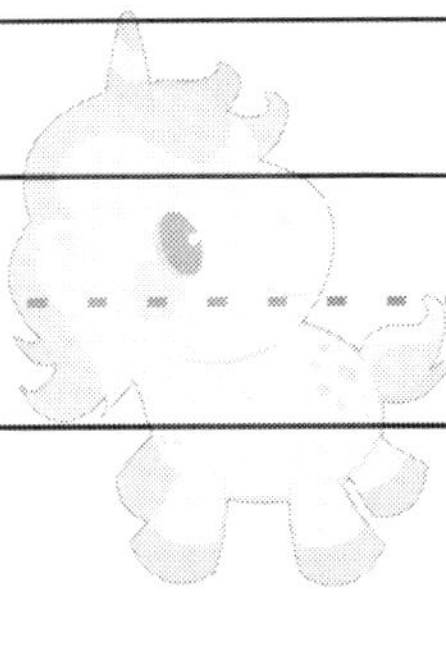

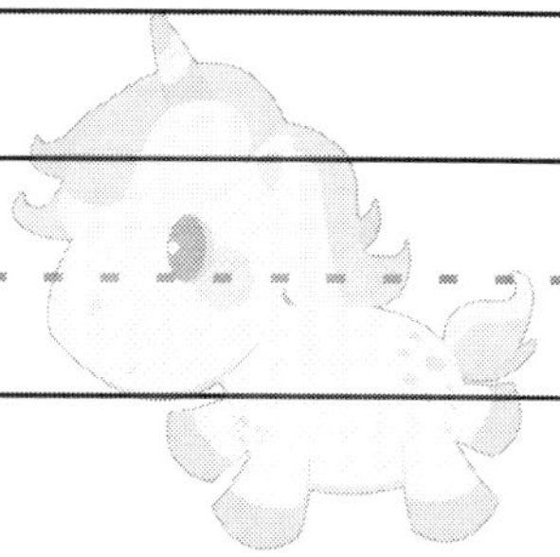

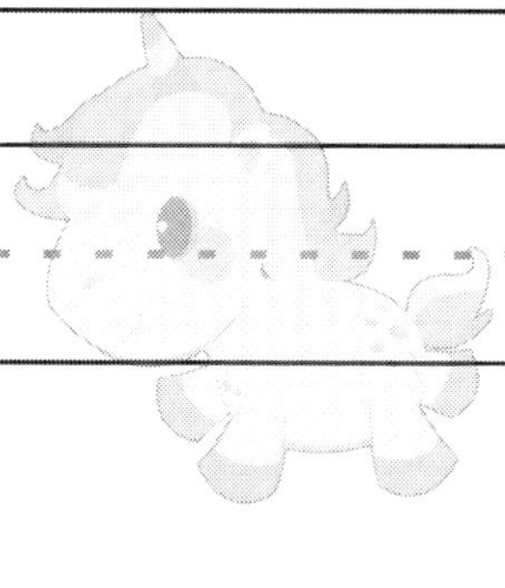

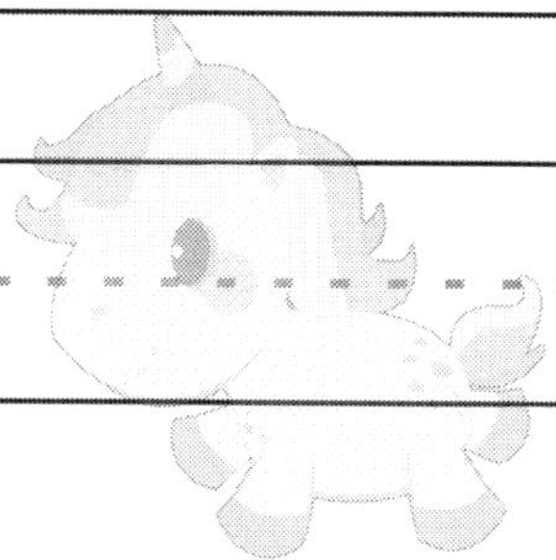

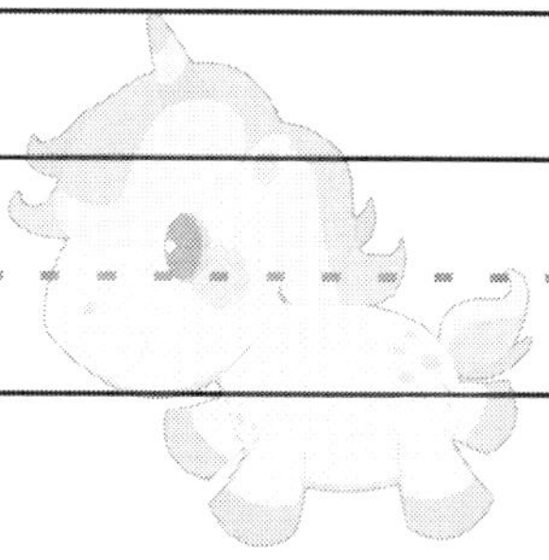

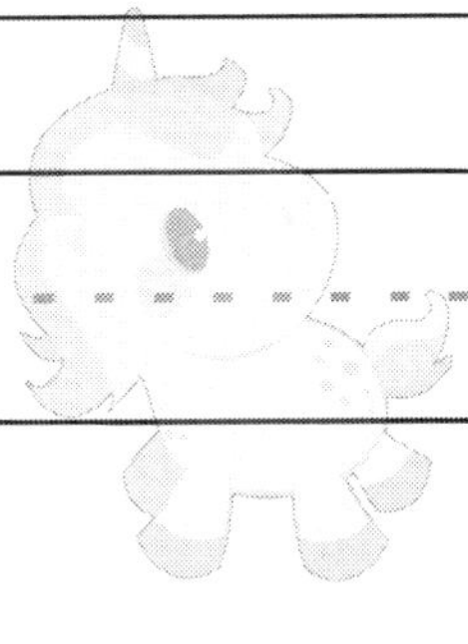

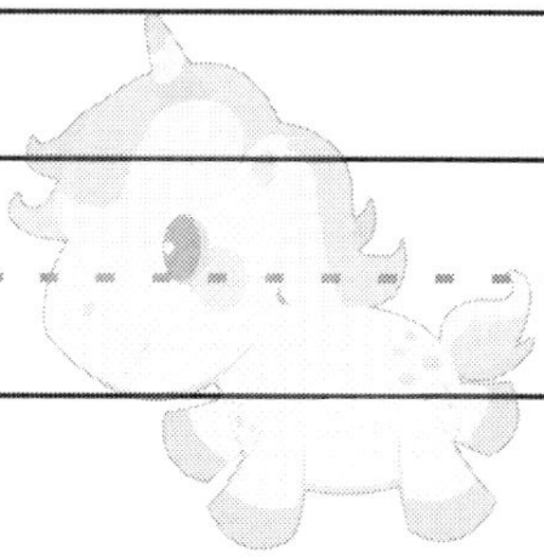

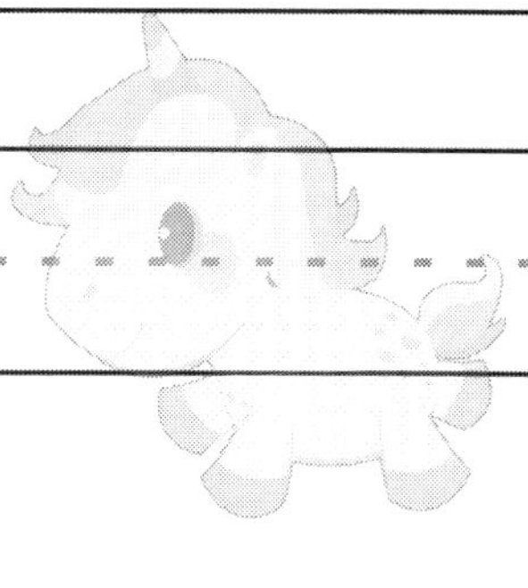

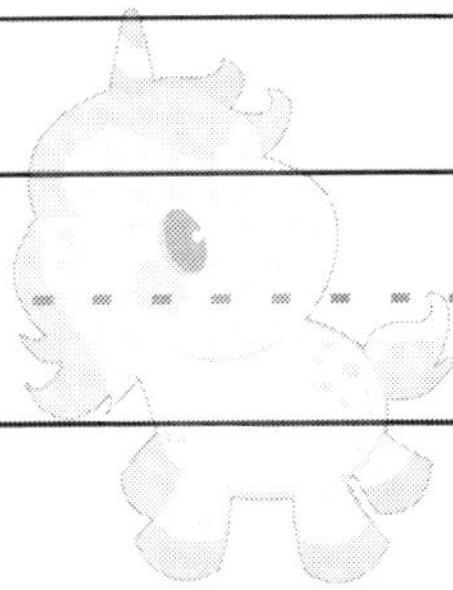

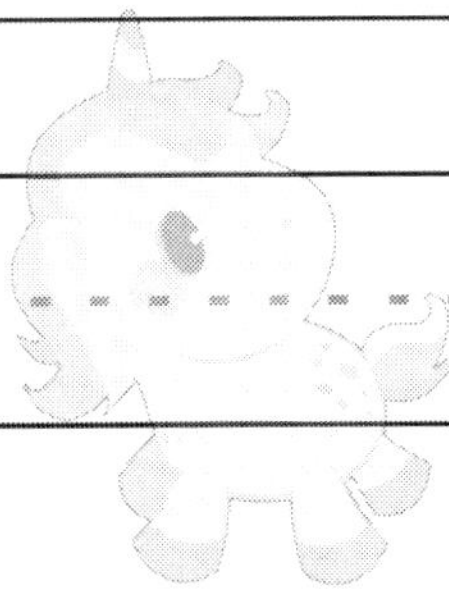

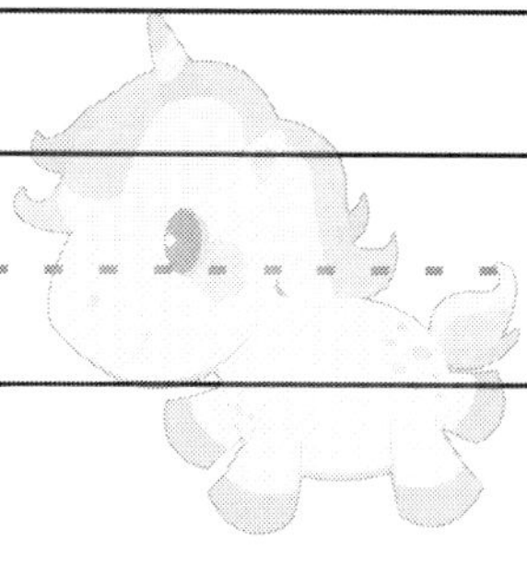

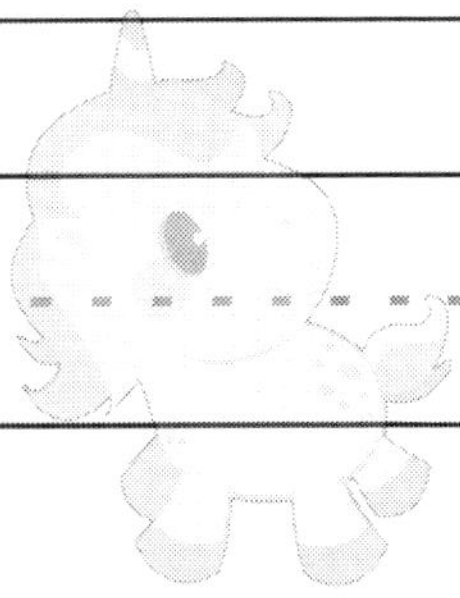

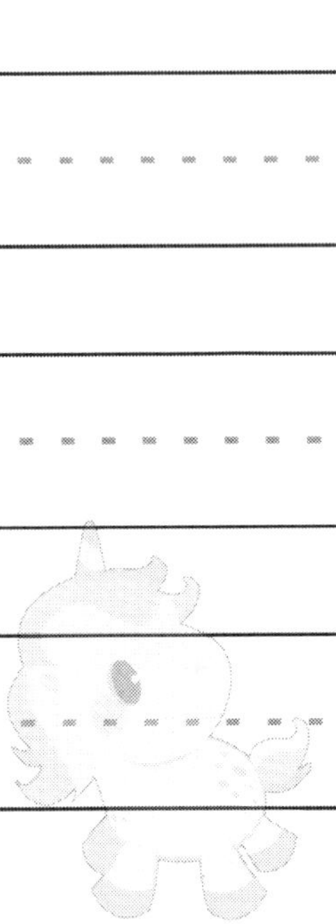

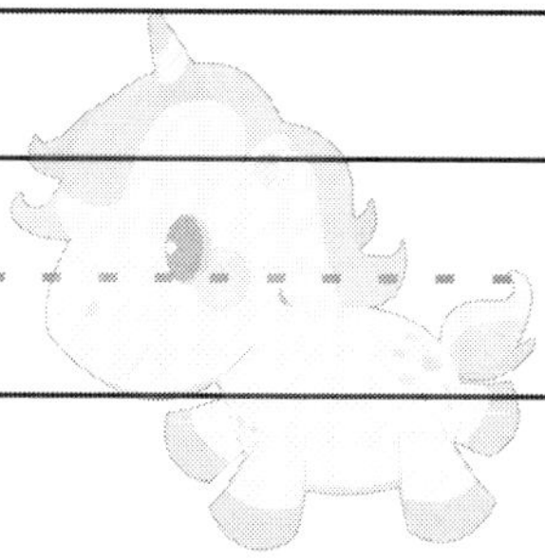

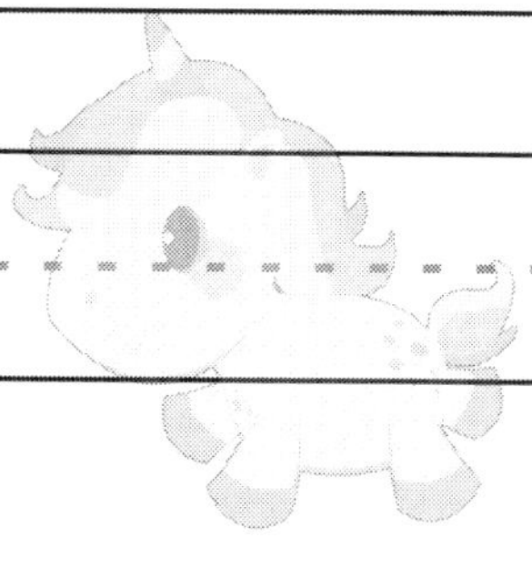

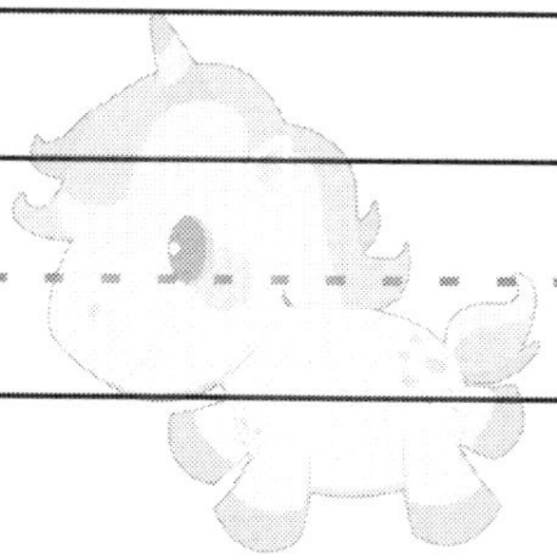

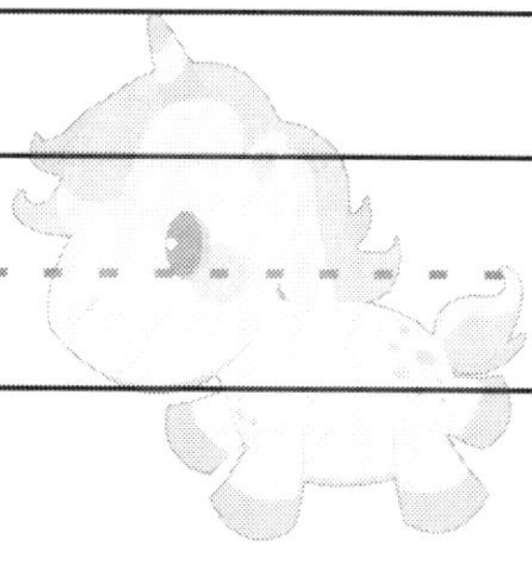

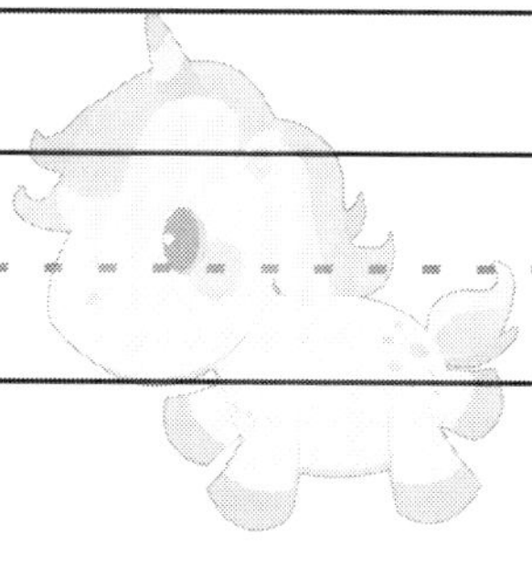

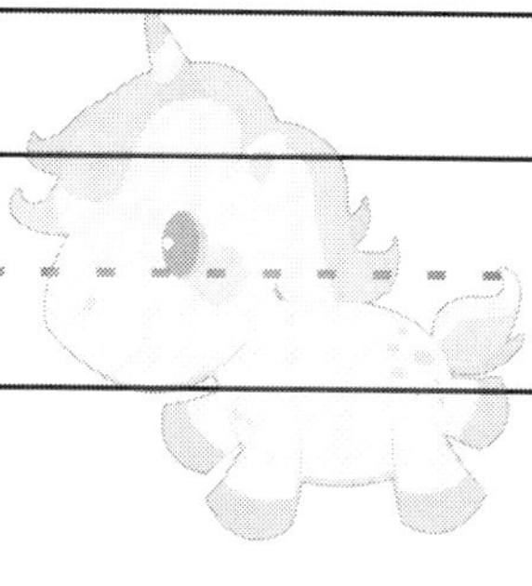

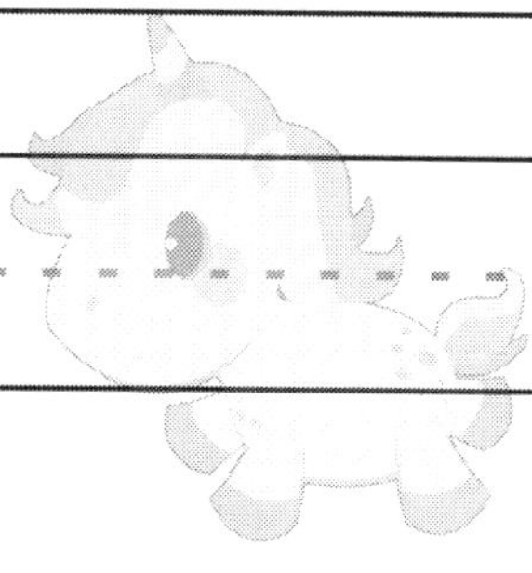

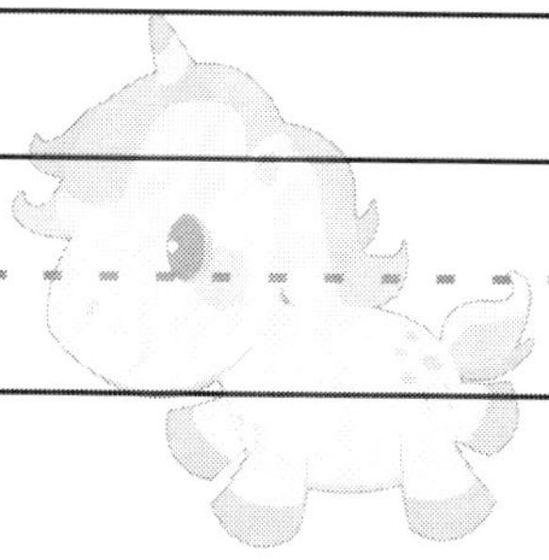

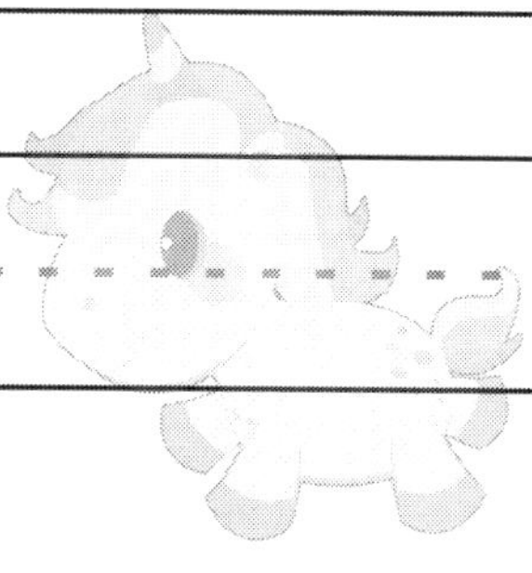

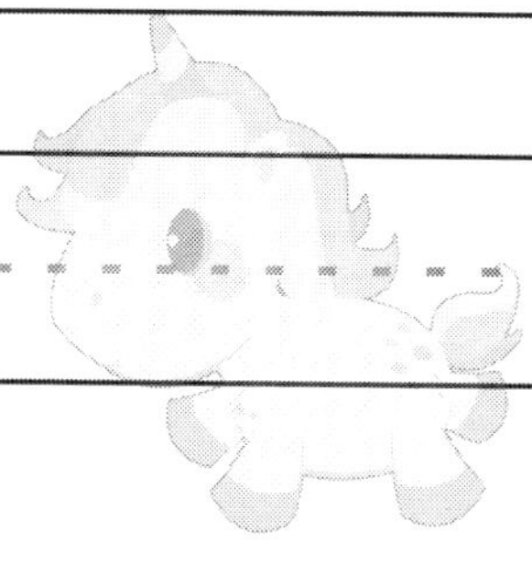

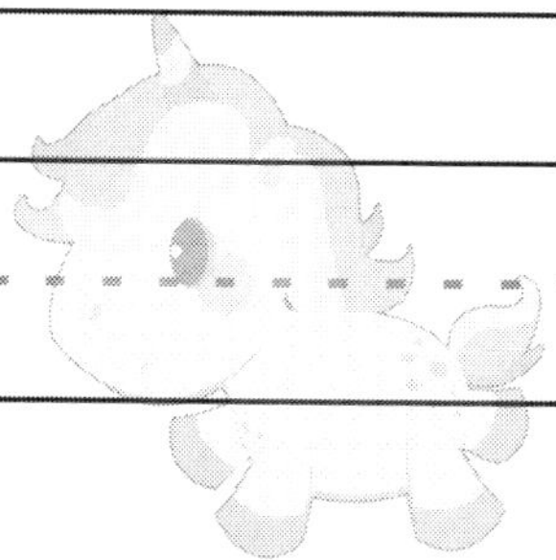

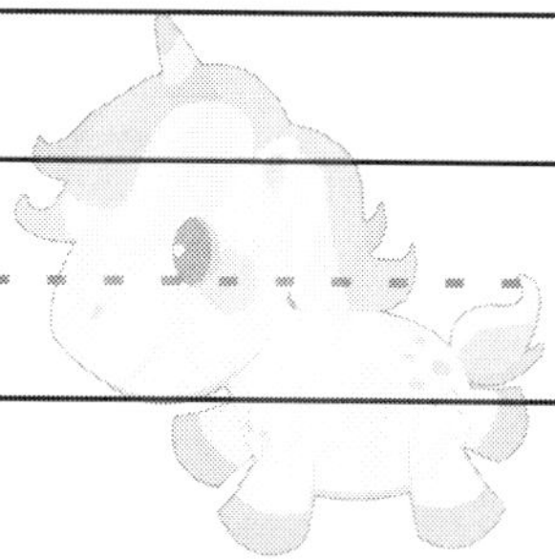

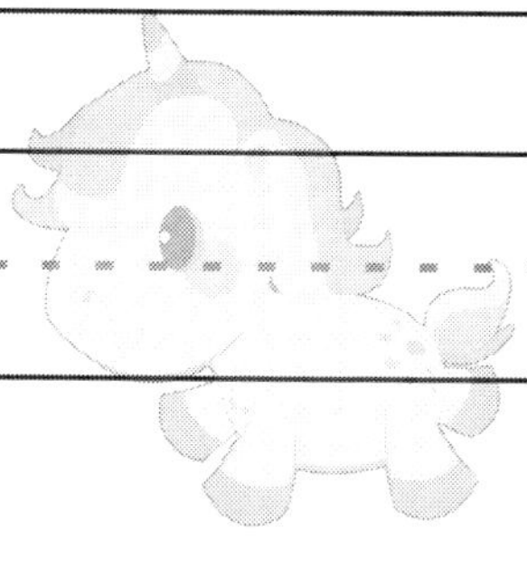

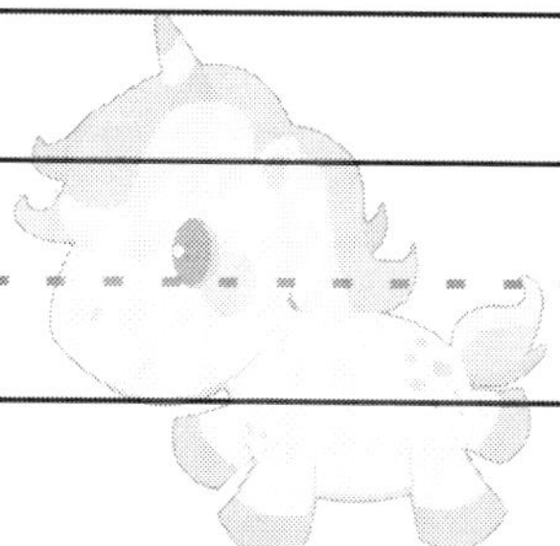

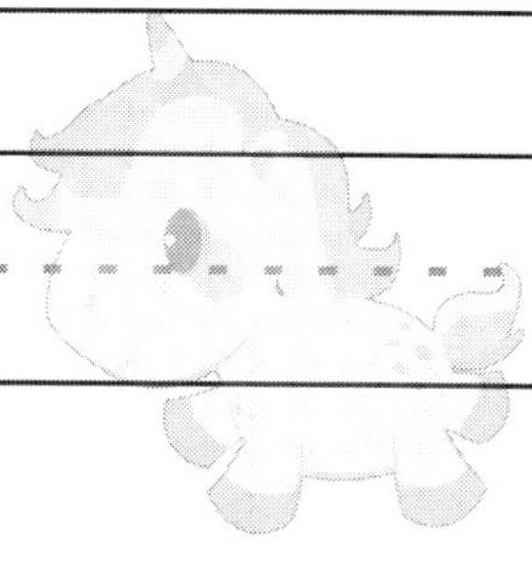

Made in the USA
Middletown, DE
06 September 2023

38005492R00062